Crocodiles

Crocodiles

A Carolrhoda Nature Watch Book

by Sally M. Walker

Carolrhoda Books, Inc. / Minneapolis

CONTENTS

Carolrhoda Books, Inc.
A division of Lerner Publishing Group
241 First Avenue North
Minneapolis, MN 55401 U.S.A.

Website address: www.lernerbooks.com

Library of Congress Cataloging-in-Publication Data

Walker, Sally M.
   Crocodiles / by Sally M. Walker.
     p.   cm. — (Nature watch)
    Summary: Describes the physical characteristics, life cycle, and behavior of crocodiles, as well as efforts to protect them.
    Includes bibliographical references (p.   ).
    ISBN: 1–57505–345–4 (lib. bdg. : alk. paper)
    1. Crocodiles—Juvenile literature. 2. Endangered species—Juvenile literature. [1. Crocodiles. 2. Endangered species.]
   I. Title. II. Series: Nature watch (Minneapolis, Minn.)
QL666.C925 W34 2004
597.98—dc21   2002151430

Manufactured in the United States of America
1 2 3 4 5 6 – JR – 09 08 07 06 05 04

With only the top of its snout showing, it is easy for this crocodile to hide from other animals.

A WATERY AMBUSH

As the sun sets over a swamp, an antelope stands on a riverbank. After looking around for signs of danger, it lowers its head for a drink. Not far away, two nostrils and a pair of shiny eyes poke slightly above the water's surface. Slowly and silently they move toward the antelope. Suddenly the water explodes as a large crocodile lunges up and out of the water. Before the antelope can lift its head, the crocodile's powerful jaws snap shut on its nose. The crocodile jerks its head, rolls its body, and pulls the antelope under the water. The skillful ambush has paid off with dinner.

Crocodiles have fascinated people for thousands of years. Aborigines, the native people of Australia, drew rock paintings of crocodiles 30,000 years ago. Three thousand years ago, the walls of Egyptian tombs were carved with pictures of a god the ancient Egyptians called Sobek. Sobek had a human body and a crocodile's head. Mummies of crocodiles and their eggs have been found in ancient Egyptian tombs. The Egyptians even had a city called Crocodilopolis.

Halfway across the world, in Mexico, the ancient Olmec people also had a crocodile god. They believed crocodiles were a sign that the harvest would be good.

The word *crocodile* comes from the Greek word *krokodeilos*, which means lizard. Crocodiles and other reptiles that are closely related to crocodiles make up a group called the crocodilians. Crocodilians have lived in and near Earth's waterways for more than 200 million years.

Many ancient crocodilians had longer legs than modern crocodiles, but the body shapes of each are very similar.

Some ancient crocodiles were enormous. *Sarcosuchus imperator*, a crocodilian that lived 110 million years ago, caught and ate dinosaurs. *Sarcosuchus imperator* grew at least 40 feet long (12 m)—about the length of a school bus!

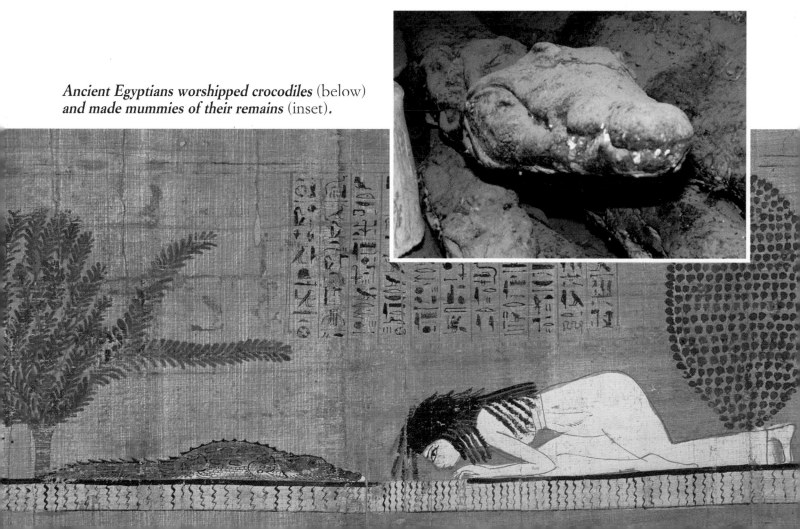

Ancient Egyptians worshipped crocodiles (below) *and made mummies of their remains* (inset).

Scientists know about these crocodilians from studying their **fossils**, or hardened remains. Many ancient crocodilians lived near water. When they died, their bones were buried in mud, then slowly turned into stone fossils. By studying the fossils, scientists have learned how crocodiles evolved, or changed over time.

The kinds of crocodilians that still exist first appeared on Earth 55 to 60 million years ago. Modern crocodilians include crocodiles, alligators, caimans, and gharials (also called gavials).

Scientists classify, or sort, animals into large groups called families. Family members share many similarities in appearance. Crocodiles belong to the family Crocodylidae.

Caimans are closely related to crocodiles but do not belong to the Crocodylidae family.

Crocodiles Around the World

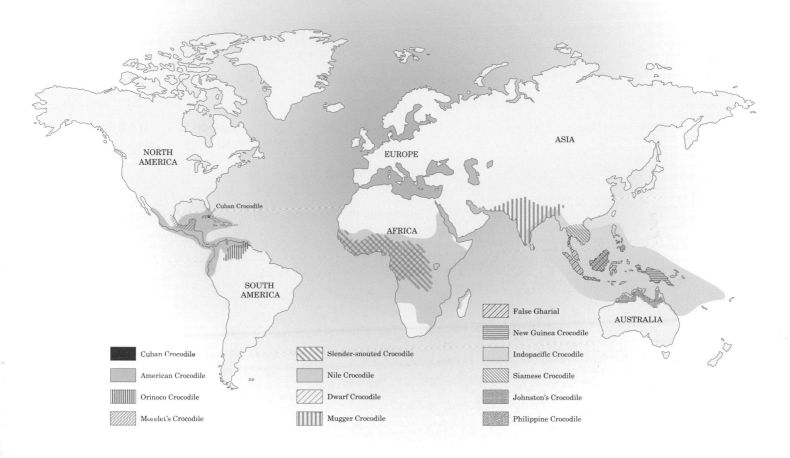

Cuban Crocodile	
American Crocodile	
Orinoco Crocodile	
Morelet's Crocodile	
Slender-snouted Crocodile	
Nile Crocodile	
Dwarf Crocodile	
Mugger Crocodile	
False Gharial	
New Guinea Crocodile	
Indopacific Crocodile	
Siamese Crocodile	
Johnston's Crocodile	
Philippine Crocodile	

Scientists further classify crocodiles into smaller groups called species. Animals within a species are even more alike than animals grouped in a family. Animals of the same species are able to mate with each other and produce young. There are 14 species of crocodiles.

Crocodiles live in the waters of every continent except Europe and Antarctica. Only one species, the American crocodile, lives in the United States. It is found in the southern tip of Florida.

Crocodiles live in **tropical** places, where the temperature remains warm or hot year-round. They can be found in a wide variety of watery environments. Most crocodiles stay in freshwater. They live in lakes, rivers, ponds, swamps, and even water-filled ditches that people have dug to water crops.

Indopacific crocodiles, like the three swimming here, are also known as "saltwater crocodiles" because they can live in both freshwater and saltwater.

Since crocodiles often rest with only their nostrils and eyes showing above the water's surface, they prefer still water or water that flows slowly. Fast-flowing water and water with waves can flood a crocodile's nostrils. That makes breathing difficult.

Crocodiles such as New Guinea crocodiles, muggers, and false gharials rarely, if ever, go in areas where the water is salty. But other crocodiles are able to tolerate **brackish**, or slightly salty, water.

American and Indopacific crocodiles often live in coastal areas such as swamps. They easily survive in brackish water and can even live in ocean water for long periods of time. That's why some people use the name saltwater crocodile, or "salties," instead of the name Indopacific crocodile. Indopacific crocodiles often swim to offshore islands. They have been found swimming several miles out to sea.

A flap of skin in a crocodile's mouth keeps water out of its lungs, so it is able to swim with its mouth open.

PHYSICAL CHARACTERISTICS

Crocodiles are perfectly built for spending a lot of time in the water. That may be one reason why crocodiles' bodies have remained basically the same shape for millions of years. The crocodile's long, streamlined body glides easily through the water. Its nostrils are on the end of its long snout, or nose, so it can breathe while most of its body is underwater.

Crocodiles have no lips, so their mouths can't close completely. Water trickles in and out of the mouth whenever the crocodile is underwater. For many animals, including humans, this would be a problem. Breathing through nostrils above the water at the same time the mouth is open underwater is dangerous for most animals. Water could flow into the lungs. If that happened, an animal could drown. The inside of the crocodile's mouth has **adapted**, or changed over thousands of years, so this doesn't happen. A fold of skin at the back of the mouth closes down to meet a fold on the back of the tongue. The tight seal prevents water from flowing into the crocodile's lungs.

A crocodile's skin is protected by tough scales called **scutes**. Crocodile scutes do not overlap each other, like the scales on a fish or a snake do. The crocodile sheds scutes one at a time, when they wear out. Bony plates called **osteoderms** provide extra protection for the crocodile. Osteoderms are embedded in the crocodile's skin along its back. Some crocodiles also have osteoderms along their bellies. Even though crocodile skin is tough, crocodiles must still watch out for animals with sharp teeth and claws.

A crocodile's skin is protected by tough scales (scutes) and bony projections (osteoderms).

The African dwarf crocodile is the smallest species of crocodile.

The 14 species of crocodiles vary in size. The Indopacific crocodile is the largest. Full-grown males can grow as long as 23 feet (7 m), about the width of a two-car garage. However, Indopacific crocodiles aren't usually found longer than about 17 feet (5 m), a little longer than a minivan. The largest Indopacific crocodiles can weigh more than 2,000 pounds (1,000 kg). American and Orinoco crocodiles also grow quite large—up to 19 or 20 feet (6 m) long.

Morelet's, Johnston's, and Philippine crocodiles are among the smaller species. They usually reach lengths of 8 to 10 feet (about 3 m), a little longer than a picnic table. The African dwarf crocodile is the smallest. It grows to a maximum length of about 6 feet (slightly less than 2 m).

This crocodile's belly is a lighter color than the rest of its body.

Crocodiles have different coloring, depending on species. Most are varying shades of brown. A crocodile's belly is often a lighter color than the rest of its body—usually yellowish or tan. No matter what the species, a crocodile's color is frequently a shade of brown that best blends in with its surroundings. For example, Indopacific crocodiles living in India may be a different shade of brown than Indopacific crocodiles living in Australia.

When a crocodile opens its mouth, the first thing people usually notice is the sharp teeth. Even when a crocodile's mouth appears to be shut, some of its pointed teeth are still visible. Most of a crocodile's teeth are **canines**. Canines are pointed teeth designed to stab deeply and quickly into **prey**, or the animals that crocodiles hunt.

Even a crocodile's molars, the teeth at the back of its mouth, are pointed. They are good for crushing prey. A crocodile's jaws snap together with bone-crushing force. And once a crocodile's teeth sink in, they don't often let go.

Crocodiles have 28 to 32 teeth in their lower jaw. The upper jaw has 30 to 40 teeth. The exact number of teeth in each jaw depends on the species of crocodile. As a tooth becomes dull or worn out, a new tooth forms below it. The new tooth grows up into the soft inner part of the old one. Soon the old tooth loosens and falls out. By that time the new tooth is in place and ready to bite.

Crocodiles' mouths are full of pointed, fearsome-looking teeth.

The shape of a crocodile's snout is one of the physical characteristics scientists use to tell crocodile species apart. Morelet's, Siamese, and Philippine crocodiles have broad snouts. Other crocodiles, such as false gharial, Orinoco, African slender-snouted, and Johnston's, have slender snouts.

Both wide and slender snouts clamp down with tremendous force. The muscles that close a crocodile's jaws are very thick and powerful. A large crocodile chomps down with enough force to crush almost anything caught between its jaws. Once they snap shut, it's difficult for a prey animal to escape.

Anatomy of a Crocodile

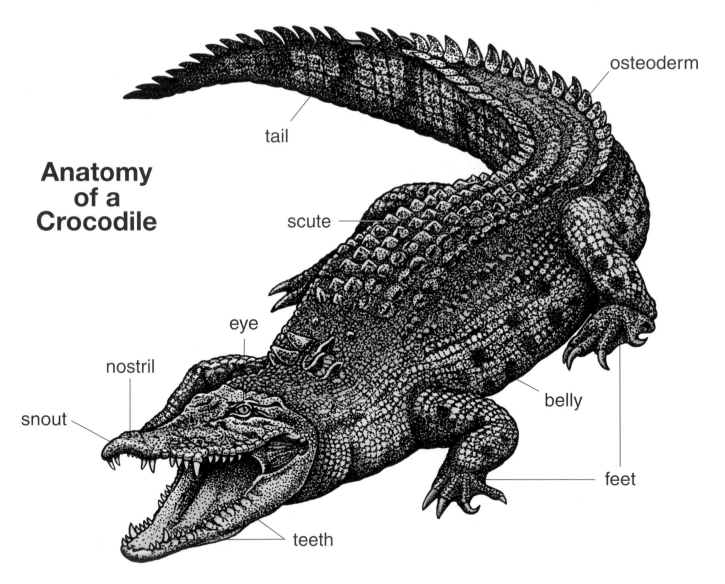

osteoderm

tail

scute

eye

nostril

snout

belly

feet

teeth

Crocodiles are most comfortable in water but also move well on land.

CROCODILES AND THEIR WORLD

Crocodiles spend a lot of time in the water. But their survival also depends on having warm, dry land nearby.

On land, a crocodile may not appear as graceful as it does in the water. But it doesn't have any trouble getting where it's going. Crocodiles can travel on land at various speeds. The slowest speed is called a high walk. During a high walk, the crocodile lifts its body high off the ground by straightening its legs. A crocodile can high walk very slowly or travel at a speed of up to 3 miles an hour (5 km/h). That's about as fast as a person walks when she is walking steadily.

If a crocodile on land is startled, it may collapse onto its chest and belly with its limbs out to the sides. In this position, it swings its limbs and thrashes its body side to side, sliding along on its belly. This is called a belly crawl. Crocodiles usually belly crawl to make quick dashes into the water.

Crocodiles are at home swimming in the water.

Some crocodiles can gallop. A galloping crocodile would never win a race with a horse, but it can reach speeds close to 11 miles per hour (17 km/h). Really large crocodiles seldom gallop. They're just too heavy and awkward. Smaller crocodiles, such as Johnston's crocodiles, gallop across sand and grass fairly often. A frightened, galloping crocodile usually heads straight toward water, where it can swim gracefully.

Once it is in the water, the crocodile is truly at home. When a crocodile swims, its powerful tail sweeps back and forth in an S-shaped motion. To make gliding through the water even easier, a crocodile holds its legs close to its body. If the crocodile decides to change direction, it spreads the toes of one of its webbed feet. The foot acts like a boat's rudder and helps steer the crocodile's body.

Even though only its eyes and nose poke up above the water, a crocodile knows what is going on nearby. Crocodiles have excellent eyesight and are often on the lookout for their next meal. Crocodile eyes are set closely together. Their close placement allows a crocodile to judge precisely where its prey is. That makes capture more likely.

Crocodiles see well in daylight and in darkness. A layer of cells inside each eye called the **tapetum** helps them see at night. The tapetum reflects light rays. When light enters a crocodile's eye, the tapetum reflects the rays inside the eye. The reflected rays make everything appear brighter. That makes seeing in the dark easier.

Crocodiles have excellent eyesight.

Crocodiles' eyes glow in the dark because light is reflected from the tapetum.

The reflected light also makes a crocodile's eyes glow in the dark, just like a cat's eyes do. When people travel at night in crocodile territory, they often shine lights on the water. If they see two glowing circles, they know to watch out—crocodiles are near!

When a crocodile doesn't want to be seen it dips beneath the water. A thin tissue called a **nictitating membrane** covers the crocodile's eyes. The nictitating membrane protects the crocodile's eyes, almost like a clear eyelid. The crocodile's vision is blurred when the membrane covers the eye. But enough light passes through to allow the crocodile to see where it is swimming.

Crocodiles don't just rely on their eyesight. A keen sense of smell helps them locate prey. Their nostrils breathe in lots of smells that provide information on what kinds of animals are in the area.

Sneaking up on a crocodile wouldn't be easy, since crocodiles have sharp hearing. A flap of tissue protects a crocodile's ears when it sinks beneath the water's surface. The flap closes down over the ear opening and prevents water from flowing in.

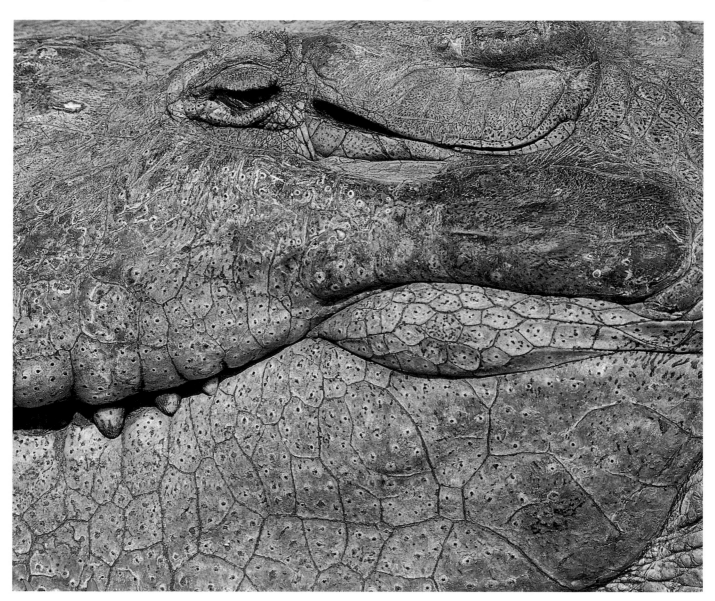

A flap of tissue protects a crocodile's ear when it is underwater.

Crocodiles spend much of their time alone.

DAILY ROUTINE AND COMMUNICATIONS

Crocodiles spend most of their time resting, either in the water or on land. Often, they remain alone. Dominant males usually have a **territory** they defend from other males. A dominant, or large and mature, male does not want other males to have access to the females and food sources in his territory. Some female crocodiles also have territories.

Crocodiles are **cold-blooded** animals. This means their blood temperature rises and falls with the temperature of the air or water that surrounds them.

Since crocodiles are cold-blooded, they must take care not to let their bodies get too cold or too hot. Crocodiles control heat loss and gain in several ways. In the morning, when the sun rises, a crocodile may leave the water and **bask** in the sun. The sun's heat warms the crocodile's body. Basking is more common during the winter months, when cool night temperatures lower the temperature of the crocodile's body.

In the summer, daytime air temperatures can become very hot in tropical places. If a crocodile lies in the hot sun for too long, its body will overheat. The crocodile could get sick or even die. So during the summer, crocodiles spend more of the daylight hours submerged in the cooler water. They may climb out onto land during the night, after the sun has set and the air temperature has dropped.

These crocodiles are cooling down in muddy water.

Crocodiles can communicate by roaring like a lion.

A crocodile's heart also helps it control body heat. The heart moves blood through the body very efficiently. During cool periods, the heart can reduce the amount of blood that flows toward the outer surfaces of the body. That keeps most of the blood near the crocodile's organs, helping keep the crocodile warm. If the crocodile gets too warm, it can pump blood into its osteoderms. The blood carries heat away from the crocodile's organs to the surface of its body, where the heat is lost. This keeps the crocodile cool.

As part of their daily routine, crocodiles communicate with each other about many things. Their communication may be loud, soft, or even silent. Young crocodiles are very vocal. They cry for their mother's help whenever they are frightened. An adult crocodile can growl and roar like a lion.

When one crocodile enters another crocodile's territory, the newcomer may be greeted by a fierce roar. The roar lets the newcomer know it is considered a trespasser. If the warning is ignored, a chase or even a fight may follow.

A crocodile can communicate by using its body instead of its mouth. **Head slaps** are among the most common body signals. To make a head slap, a crocodile lifts its head slightly out of the water. It opens its mouth wide. Then the crocodile swiftly lowers its head. Its jaws snap shut with a loud pop just as the lower jaw smacks the water's surface with a loud crack. The sudden noise of a head slap is impossible to ignore. Crocodiles may head slap just to let other crocodiles know they are there or to warn other crocodiles to stay out of their territory. They also may head slap to signal that they are ready to mate.

Crocodiles sometimes use body language to communicate with each other.

While in the water, crocodiles can communicate using infrasound.

Crocodiles also use sound to communicate in a way that humans can barely hear or may not hear at all. With its body just covered with water, a crocodile sometimes contracts, or tightens, the muscles in the trunk of its body. The muscle contractions cause very low-toned sounds to spread out from its body. The sounds are called infrasound. Infrasound is noise lower than humans are usually able to hear. Sometimes the infrasound can be heard by humans. If it can, it sounds like the rumbling of faraway thunder. Depending on the species, crocodiles use infrasound during courtship, to warn other crocodiles of their presence, or to alert their young in times of danger.

Crocodiles communicate silently as well. Scent glands near the chin and other parts of the body leave silent messages. By rubbing its scent glands along a log or another surface, a crocodile leaves its scent behind. The scent may drive away **predators**, attract mates, or mark a crocodile's territory.

Some crocodiles communicate with each other by blowing bubbles when they are ready to mate.

Slender-snouted crocodiles eat fish head first so they are not hurt by the fish's scales.

HUNTING AND DIET

Crocodiles prey on a wide variety of animals. Most crocodiles will eat whatever they can catch. That includes birds, insects, snakes, snails, turtles, frogs, and sometimes people.

The shape of the crocodile's snout usually gives a good clue as to what type of food it eats. Thin, narrow snouts, such as those found on African slender-snouted crocodiles and false gharials, usually indicate a diet that includes a lot of fish. Narrow snouts cut smoothly through the water and quickly snatch up fish. But the thinner snout is more fragile than a wider one, so these crocodiles usually don't eat animals that could fight hard and possibly harm the snout.

Nile and Indopacific crocodiles and muggers have much broader snouts. They eat mostly land animals, some of which can be very large. Nile crocodiles will eat animals as large as buffalo and wildebeests.

If they are hungry and prey is available, crocodiles will hunt at any time of day. But most species, especially the New Guinea and American croco- diles, prefer to hunt at night. Crocodiles are sabotage hunters. That means they hide, then sneak up and ambush their prey. At first the crocodile remains submerged, with only its eyes and nostrils showing. Prey is fooled into thinking there is no danger. But as soon as the prey gets within striking distance—*wham*! The crocodile explodes into action.

This crocodile is sneaking up on its prey.

When crocodiles attack prey, they can charge out of the water, if necessary. But they usually don't run after prey if they don't have to. Running uses up a lot of energy. Cold-blooded animals can't make and store large amounts of energy. So crocodiles usually wait for prey to come near.

Sometimes, a crocodile uses its head to swipe at the legs of large prey. While the prey is off balance, the crocodile has more time to grab it. With its jaws tightly clamped, the crocodile drowns large prey by dragging it into deep water. Then the crocodile spins itself, like a rolling log, until a mouthful tears from the prey's body. If the prey is large enough, the crocodile that kills it will usually share the kill with other crocodiles. When several crocodiles grab onto large prey, some hold the body in place while another spins and rolls to tear off a chunk. Crocodiles take turns doing this, so all get a portion of a large kill.

These crocodiles are sharing an impala carcass.

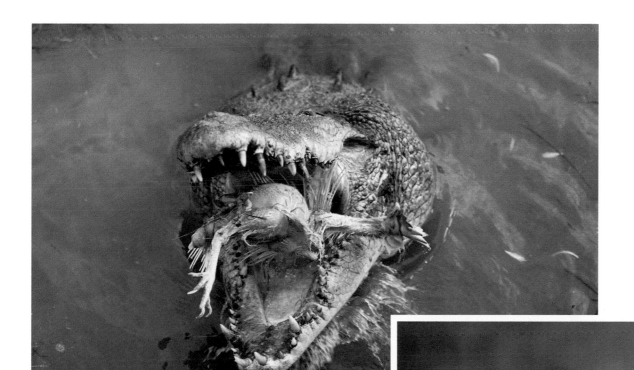

Crocodiles are ferocious eaters (above). *They cannot chew, so they tilt back their heads and swallow big chunks of food whole* (right).

When people eat, they use the flat molars at the back of their mouths to grind and chew food. Crocodiles can't chew. Their bottom jaw can't move sideways like a person's does when she chews. Since crocodiles can't chew, they either swallow prey whole or, if the prey is large, tear off a chunk. When the crocodile is ready to swallow, it tips its head upward and opens its jaws. The food falls toward the back of the mouth and the crocodile gulps it down.

Gastroliths in a crocodile's stomach help it digest the hard horns and hooves of some of its prey.

After a crocodile eats, its stomach digests, or removes the nutrients from, its meal. Like birds, crocodiles swallow stones to help with the digestion process. Inside a crocodile's stomach, the stones, called **gastroliths**, grind the food. As a crocodile digests its food, the gastroliths crush bones, turtle shells, and other hard things the crocodile has eaten. Stomach acids dissolve the bone and shell pieces. In this way, the acids and gastroliths make more of the nutrients in the meal available to the crocodile. Some nutrients are stored as fat. Crocodiles can store large amounts of fat in their massive tails. They also have fat deposits in their abdomen and in places on their back.

At one time, people believed crocodiles were eating machines. They thought crocodiles ate lots of food every day. But scientists have discovered that this isn't true. In fact, a large crocodile, such as a Nile crocodile, may eat as few as 50 large meals per year. Many of those meals are eaten during the spring and summer months, when the sun's stronger heat better warms a crocodile's body as it basks on land. Then a crocodile has more energy for hunting.

Sometimes prey is unavailable. If necessary, crocodiles can fast, or go for long periods of time without eating. In hot seasons, a Johnston's crocodile may not eat for three to four months. Some crocodiles have gone without a meal for longer than a year. The reason a crocodile can fast is because it can live off the fat it has stored in its body.

Crocodiles hunt more often in warm weather.

This crocodile is patrolling its territory.

LIFE CYCLE

As crocodiles grow older and larger, they become ready to mate and have young. The length of the crocodile seems to be as important as its age in determining if it is ready to mate. Male muggers are ready to mate when they are about 10 years old, or about 8 feet (3 m) long. Female muggers are ready at about 6 years, when they are around 6 feet (2 m) long. Male Indopacific crocodiles mate when they are about 16 years old and 11 feet (3 m) long. Female Indopacific crocodiles are ready to mate by 12 years, when they are about 8 feet (2 m) long.

During **breeding season**, or the time of year when crocodiles mate, a male becomes much more protective of his territory and the female crocodiles in it. A dominant male may swim or walk along the boundaries of his territory. Younger males trying to enter the territory are threatened with a gaping mouth, showing all the sharp teeth. If that doesn't drive away a younger male, the two crocodiles may begin **head bashing**.

To head bash, the crocodiles stand close together. They face in the same direction. Each crocodile swings its head sideways away from the other. Then both swing their heads back the other way until they bash together. Usually, several strong bashes from the dominant male are enough to drive away the younger crocodile. Sometimes, though, males fight over territory. Then they may bite each other. Most fights don't end in death. But large cuts are common.

Sometimes crocodiles show their sharp teeth.

Crocodiles rub against each other when they are ready to mate.

Crocodiles that are ready to mate signal each other in several ways. The signals vary, depending on the species. They may raise their heads at each other, showing their soft throats. Rubbing heads and bodies together is also common. Sometimes crocodiles blow bubbles in the water. They often swim in circles around one another.

Depending on the species, a dominant male may mate with anywhere from 1 to 20 or more females in his territory. Crocodiles do not form permanent male-female pairs. After mating, the two crocodiles go their own separate ways.

After a female has mated, eggs begin growing inside her body. The tiny animal developing inside each egg is called an **embryo**. A **yolk sac** inside the eggshell is filled with protein and other nutrients. It nourishes the embryo as it grows.

Muggers may lay two **clutches**, or groups, of eggs per breeding season. But most other species lay one clutch a year. Morelet's crocodiles often lay their eggs inside nests on mats of floating vegetation. Most other crocodiles seek a place farther from the water. If water floods a nest, the embryos inside the eggs may drown. Using her strong hind legs, the female digs a hole in the sand. Crocodiles lay from 20 to 80 eggs, depending on the species.

After laying her eggs, the female covers them with sand, mud, or plants. While the eggs are incubating, or developing, the mother usually stays near the nest and guards it. Some species of crocodiles, such as Johnston's crocodiles, leave the nest unattended until just before the eggs hatch. Raccoons, lizards, and birds often eat crocodile eggs. Some people collect them.

This female crocodile is guarding her nest.

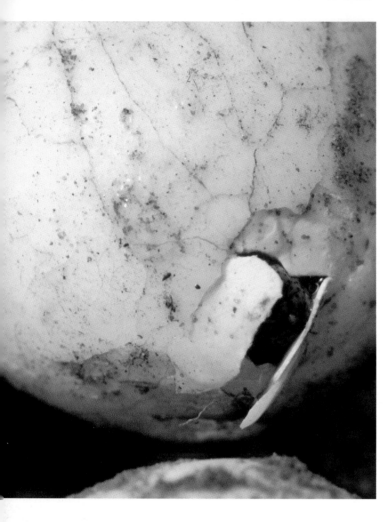

A baby crocodile is starting to hatch out of its egg.

For most animals, an embryo's sex is determined as soon as the embryo forms. This isn't true for crocodiles. The sex of a crocodile embryo is determined by the temperature that surrounds the egg as it develops.

Because crocodiles live in tropical areas, their eggs incubate at temperatures between 82°F and 93°F (28–34°C). Eggs that incubate at the coolest of these temperatures, between about 82°F and 88°F (28–31°C), become females. Eggs that incubate at the highest temperatures, between about 92°F and 93°F (33–34°C), also usually become females. Males usually develop in eggs that incubate at temperatures in the middle, between about 88°F and 92°F (31–33°C). Small variations in temperature—even less than one degree—are enough to change the sex of the developing embryo.

The eggs are ready to hatch in 55 to 90 days, depending on the species. All the eggs in a clutch hatch on the same night. The baby crocodiles are called **hatchlings**. Hatchlings cry out while they are hatching. Their *bee-yoo, bee-yoo* cries prompt their mother into action. Using her front claws, she uncovers the hatching eggs. She often helps a hatchling crack out of its shell. She gently picks up the egg with her teeth. Carefully, she rolls it between her tongue and the roof of her mouth. This cracks the shell without harming the hatchling.

After they have all hatched, the female—or sometimes the male—takes them to the water. Hatchlings from the same clutch stay together once they are in the water. They cry out to one another to keep the group together. They may bask on rocks or logs or even on their mother's back. For the first month or so, they don't stray far from their mother. And if something upsets a hatchling, it chirps out a distress call that quickly brings an adult to its aid.

After the hatchlings leave their eggs (top), *the mother gathers them in her mouth* (bottom) *and takes them to the water.*

This young crocodile is about to catch a meal.

A hatchling doesn't have to catch a meal right after it hatches. It can survive for as long as 4 months without a meal. Nutrients from the yolk sac it consumed inside its egg continue to nourish the hatchling, even after it has hatched.

Hatchlings of all crocodile species eat insects, snails, and small fish and mammals. When crocodiles are less than a year old, they don't have gastroliths. Because their prey is small, they don't need the grinding help gastroliths provide. As the young crocodiles grow larger, they seek larger prey such as turtles, crabs, frogs, snakes, and mammals. The larger a crocodile gets, the less likely it is to hunt for small prey. The energy it takes to catch small prey isn't worth spending.

Female, and sometimes male, crocodiles of most species may protect their young from predators for as long as 3 years. Hatchlings are easy targets for predators such as lizards, turtles, wild pigs, and birds. Even with a parent's protection, only a small number of hatchlings, perhaps as few as two or three per clutch, will live long enough to become adults. False gharial adults don't seem to protect their hatchlings. The survival rate of this species is even lower.

By the time a crocodile is half grown, the number of animals that prey upon it is greatly reduced. Not many animals dare to challenge a crocodile's fierce bite and strong jaws. Large wildcats, such as lions or jaguars, will eat crocodiles, particularly baby crocodiles. If elephants, rhinoceroses, and hippopotamuses are protecting their babies, they will attack and sometimes kill crocodiles. Humans are the main predators of fully grown crocodiles.

A female crocodile (below) **protects her young. Hatchlings make easy prey for creatures such as raccoons** (inset).

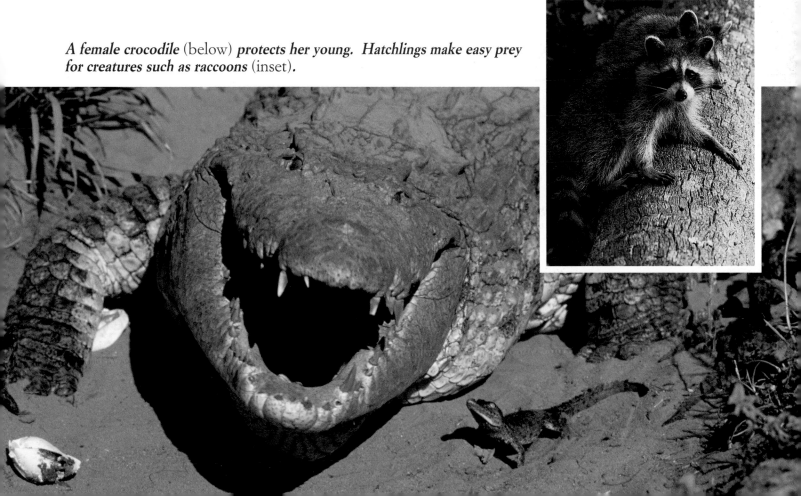

This Nile crocodile has been hunted and killed.

CROCODILES AND THE FUTURE

For 200 million years, many different species of crocodilians have crawled on the land and swum in Earth's waters. But their future existence is uncertain. Crocodiles are hunted by humans for food, for their skins, to keep as pets, and to use in trinkets such as key chains. In many countries, leather goods such as shoes, boots, and handbags made from crocodile hides have been in great demand for more than 200 years.

Starting in the 1940s, unrestricted hunting removed great numbers of adult crocodiles from the wild. And since juveniles and hatchlings were already heavily hunted in nature, few crocodiles were left to reproduce. Crocodile populations in many areas were dramatically reduced. Some populations were completely wiped out. Some species, such as the Orinoco, were hunted until they were nearly **extinct**, or no longer living.

In 1973, representatives from countries all over the world got together. They passed the Convention on International Trade on Endangered Species (CITES). CITES requires nations to outlaw trade in species that are **endangered**, or in danger of becoming extinct. Since CITES was passed, the hunting of crocodiles has been reduced.

But hunting is not the only danger crocodiles have faced. Habitat destruction, or destroying an animal's living place, also threatens crocodiles' future survival. When people build homes and other buildings, they often drain swampy crocodile habitat. Land is also drained for agricultural use. If suitable habitat and the food sources it contains are destroyed, crocodiles will not be able to survive.

Airport officials in New York have taken a lot of crocodile leather merchandise from people trying to smuggle it into the country. Since CITES was passed, trading in endangered species is illegal.

A man holds two hatchlings at a crocodile farm in India.

Some people are working to protect and preserve crocodiles for the future. They want to make sure enough crocodiles survive to breed. One way they have done this is by establishing crocodile farms.

Crocodile farms in Australia, India, and in some countries in South America have helped bring some species back from near-extinction. On these farms, crocodiles are bred, raised, and then killed for food and for their skin. Because these crocodiles are readily available for trade, it lowers the number of wild crocodiles that are killed.

Scientists also operate captive breeding programs for some species. In Venezuela, several breeding programs are trying to save the highly endangered Orinoco species. Eggs are collected from the wild. The hatchlings are fed and cared for until they are juveniles.

After several years, the juveniles are released into wildlife refuges or national parks. These are crocodile habitats that people have preserved or restored. Radio transmitters attached to the released juveniles help scientists keep track of the animals. They hope the crocodiles will survive in these protected areas.

Species such as American, Nile, and Johnston's crocodiles have done well on crocodile farms and in breeding programs. That's encouraging news. But Orinoco, Siamese, and Philippine crocodiles are still critically endangered. On the positive side, they breed well in captivity, so there is hope for the future.

People will determine if crocodiles survive on Earth or not. Crocodile farms can help ensure that enough crocodiles will be available for use in trade. Breeding programs can help replenish the number of crocodiles in captivity and in the wild. But people must enact laws to protect habitat and see that they are upheld. If we do, we can ensure that crocodile populations will be around for many years to come.

An endangered Indopacific crocodile leaps out of the water.

GLOSSARY

adapt: to change the body so an animal or plant can better survive in its environment

bask: to lie in the sun to absorb the sun's heat and warm the body

brackish: slightly salty

breeding season: a specific time of year when animals mate

canine: a large, pointed tooth used for grasping and biting

clutch: a group of eggs laid together at the same time

cold-blooded: having a body temperature that goes up and down with the surrounding temperature

embryo: a crocodile developing in its egg

endangered: in danger of becoming extinct

extinct: when all animals in a species have died out

fossil: the hardened remains of ancient life-forms

gastrolith: a stone that is swallowed and remains in the stomach. Gastroliths help crocodiles digest food by grinding it.

hatchling: a baby crocodile, recently out of its egg

head bashing: when two crocodiles bash their heads together, usually to establish dominance in a territory

head slap: a noise a crocodile makes by slapping its head against the water. Its jaws snap shut with a loud pop just as the lower jaw smacks the water's surface with a loud crack.

nictitating membrane: a thin tissue that covers the eyeball when a crocodile swims underwater

osteoderm: a bony plate embedded in a crocodile's skin that helps protect it from injury

predator: an animal that kills and eats other animals

prey: animals that are eaten by other animals

scute: a tough scale found on a crocodile's skin

tapetum: a layer of cells in the eye that reflects light. The tapetum makes it easier to see in dim light.

territory: an area a crocodile defends from other crocodiles

tropical: places where the temperature remains warm or hot year-round

yolk sac: a protein sac that nourishes an unborn crocodile while it grows inside its egg

INDEX

ABOUT THE AUTHOR

Sally M. Walker is the author of numerous science books for children, including *Earthquakes, Manatees, Rhinos, Hippos, Sea Horses,* and *Dolphins,* all published by Carolrhoda Books. Although her favorite job is writing, Ms. Walker also works as a children's literature consultant and has taught children's literature at Northern Illinois University. While she writes, Ms. Walker is usually surrounded by her family's golden retriever and two cats, who don't say very much but provide good company. She lives in Illinois with her husband and two children.

PHOTO ACKNOWLEDGMENTS

Photographs are reproduced through the courtesy of: © Lynn Stone, cover, pp. 13, 20, 21, 27, 34, 41; © Martin Harvey; Gallo Images/CORBIS, pp. 2, 39 (top); © Raymond Cramm, Photo Researchers, pp. 4–5; © Michael S. Yamashita/CORBIS, p. 6; © Carl & Ann Purcell/CORBIS, p. 7 (inset); © Gianni Dagli Orti/CORBIS, p. 7 (bottom); © Kevin Schafer, Photo Researchers, p. 8; © Albrecht G. Schaefer/CORBIS, p. 10; © Tom McHugh, Photo Researchers, pp. 11, 24; © Jonathan Blair/CORBIS, pp. 12, 17, 38, 39 (inset), 40, 43; © Erwin and Peggy Bauer/Bruce Coleman, Inc., p. 14; © Jeffrey Rotman, Photo Researchers, pp. 15, 31 (top), 45; © Stephen Frink/CORBIS, p. 18; © Gavriel Jecan/CORBIS, p. 19; © Clive Druett; Papilio/CORBIS, p. 22; © David Katzenstein/CORBIS, p. 23; © Jeffrey L. Rotman/CORBIS, pp. 25, 42; © David B. Fleetham/Visuals Unlimited, p. 26; © Michael Dick/Animals Animals, p. 28; © John Scheiber/CORBIS, p. 29; © Darrell Gulin/CORBIS, p. 30; © Peter Johnson/CORBIS, p. 31 (bottom); © Galen Rowell/CORBIS, p. 32; © Brian A. Vikander/CORBIS, p. 33; © Joe McDonald/Visuals Unlimited, p. 35; © Fritz Prenzel/Animals Animals, p. 36; © Chinch Gryniewicz; Ecoscene/CORBIS, p. 37; © Shaen Adey; Gallo Images/CORBIS, p. 41 (bottom); © Arne Hodalic/CORBIS, p. 44. Illustrations on pp. 9 and 16 by Laura Westlund, © 2004 Carolrhoda Books, Inc.